MOROCCO

By Theia Lake and
Joanne Mattern

Published in 2025 by Cavendish Square Publishing, LLC
2544 Clinton Street, Buffalo, NY 14224

Second Edition

Website: cavendishsq.com

Library of Congress Cataloging-in-Publication Data

Names: Lake, Theia, author. | Mattern, Joanne, author.
Title: Morocco / Theia Lake and Joanne Mattern..
Description: [Buffalo] : Cavendish Square Publishing, [2025] | Series:
Exploring world cultures, second edition | Includes index.
Identifiers: LCCN 2024008667 (print) | LCCN 2024008668 (ebook) | ISBN
9781502671011 (library binding) | ISBN 9781502671004 (paperback) | ISBN
9781502671028 (ebook)
Subjects: LCSH: Morocco--Juvenile literature.
Classification: LCC DT305 .L35 2025 (print) | LCC DT305 (ebook) | DDC
964--dc23/eng/20240301
LC record available at https://lccn.loc.gov/2024008667
LC ebook record available at https://lccn.loc.gov/2024008668

Writers: Joanne Mattern; Theia Lake (second edition)
Editor: Theresa Emminizer
Copyeditor: Danielle Haynes
Designer: Andrea Davison-Bartolotta

The photographs in this book are used by permission and through the courtesy of: Cover Nadinlargo/iStockphoto.com; p. 4 xamnesiacx84/Shutterstock.com; p. 5 Just Another Photographer/Shutterstock.com; p. 6 Peter Hermes Furian/Shutterstock.com; p. 7 Ondrej Bucek/Shutterstock.com; p. 8 posztos/Shutterstock.com; p. 9 File:Muhammad V.jpg/Wikimedia Commons; p. 10 Wirestock Creators/Shutterstock.com; p. 11 Royal Graphics/Shutterstock.com; p. 12 Janusz Pienkowski/Shutterstock.com; p. 13 JackKPhoto/Shutterstock.com; p. 15 (top) Stefano Zaccaria/Shutterstock.com; p. 15 (bottom) vikee214/Shutterstock.com; p. 16 JulioRV/Shutterstock.com; p. 17 Masterovoy/Shutterstock.com; p. 19 (top) zizou7/Shutterstock.com; p. 19 (bottom) Pavel Szabo/Shutterstock.com; p. 20 Fresnel/Shutterstock.com; p. 21 younes Goussyra/Shutterstock.com; p. 22 Marko Rupena/Shutterstock.com; p. 23 Vicente Sargues/Shutterstock.com; p. 24 celiachen/Shutterstock.com; pp. 25, 28 Casablanca Stock/Shutterstock.com; p. 26 mohamed bahssine/Shutterstock.com; p. 27 Wiola Wiaderek/Shutterstock.com; p. 29 SEAGULL_L/Shutterstock.com.

CPSIA compliance information: Batch #CS25CSQ: For further information contact Cavendish Square Publishing LLC at 1-877-980-4450.

Printed in the United States of America

CONTENTS

Introduction 4
Chapter 1 Geography 6
Chapter 2 History 8
Chapter 3 Government 10
Chapter 4 The Economy 12
Chapter 5 The Environment 14
Chapter 6 The People Today 16
Chapter 7 Lifestyle 18
Chapter 8 Religion 20
Chapter 9 Language 22
Chapter 10 Arts and Festivals 24
Chapter 11 Fun and Play 26
Chapter 12 Food 28
Glossary 30
Find Out More 31
Index 32

INTRODUCTION

Morocco is a beautiful and unique, or one-of-a-kind, country. It's located, or found, in the western part of North Africa called Maghreb. Morocco is the only African country with coasts along both the Atlantic Ocean and the Mediterranean Sea. It also has many mountains in the middle.

Many colorful dyes and spices are sold in Moroccan markets.

People who make their home in Morocco are called Moroccans. Moroccans speak many different languages, including Arabic, Tamazight languages, and French. Most Moroccan people are Muslim.

Morocco has a long, interesting history. Its **culture** has been shaped by Arab, European, African, and Berber **traditions**. The Berber people are an **ethnic** group indigenous, or native to, North Africa.

The arts, music, food, and celebrations of Morocco reflect, or show, the **influences** of these different groups. It's part of what makes Morocco such a special place!

These Moroccan kids are having fun playing soccer in the city streets of Fès.

GEOGRAPHY

Morocco is a small country. It covers 172,414 square miles (446,550 square kilometers). Algeria lies along Morocco's eastern border. A territory, or piece of land, called Western Sahara lies to the south.

The Sahara, a desert, spreads across much of eastern and southern Morocco. The Moroccan part of the Sahara is the third-largest desert in the world.

The Strait of Gibraltar is a narrow waterway that separates Morocco from Spain, just 8 miles (13 km) to the north.

FACT!

The Moulouya River is an important river in Morocco. It starts in the Atlas Mountains and flows into the Mediterranean Sea.

Jebel Toubkal is the highest mountain in Morocco. It's 13,665 feet (4,165 meters) tall.

The Atlas Mountains rise in the south and continue across the eastern border. The Rif mountain range is in the north. **Fertile** plains lie between the Rif mountains and the Mediterranean Sea.

WESTERN SAHARA

Since 1975, Morocco has claimed Western Sahara as its own. However, other nations don't agree that this land is part of Morocco. Because of this, Western Sahara is called a disputed territory. Western Sahara is home to the Indigenous Sahrawi people led a group called the Polisario Front.

HISTORY

The Berbers were some of the first people to live in the area that's now Morocco. **Ancient** Romans also lived there. In 680 CE, Arabian fighters came to the area. They became the rulers of Morocco.

FACT!
Today, Muḥammad VI is king of Morocco. He is the son of King Hassan II.

These are some of the ancient ruins that still stand in Morocco today.

From the late 1400s to the 1800s, many European countries wanted to control Morocco. Morocco fought back. However, in 1912, its ruler, Sultan Abd al-Hafid, signed the Treaty of Fès. This treaty, or agreement, gave control of Morocco to France.

Morocco remained a French colony until 1956. It became independent from France on March 2, 1956.

Muḥammad V is pictured here in 1934 when he was sultan.

MUḤAMMAD V

Muḥammad V was the sultan, or ruler, of Morocco from 1927 to 1957. Muḥammad V worked to win Morocco's independence from France and Spain. After Morocco became independent, Muḥammad V kept ruling the country as king from 1957 until 1961. His son Hassan II ruled as king after him.

GOVERNMENT

Morocco's government has three branches: executive, legislative, and judicial. Rabat is the country's capital.

The king and the prime minister lead the executive branch. The prime minister oversees the laws. They also choose cabinet ministers who help lead different parts of the government, such as health care and education.

FACT!

Morocco's monarchs are all part of the same dynasty, or family line.

This is the Moroccan Parliament building in Rabat.

The legislative branch makes the laws. Members of Parliament form this branch. There are two parts of Parliament: the House of Representatives and the House of Councillors.

The judicial branch is made up of courts. The Supreme Court is the highest court in the land.

The Moroccan flag has a red background and features a green pentagram, or five-pointed star.

A PARLIAMENTARY CONSTITUTIONAL MONARCHY

Morocco's government is a parliamentary constitutional monarchy. That means there's a monarch, such as a king or queen. There's also a **constitution** and a government based on that constitution. Morocco's first constitution was written in 1962. The government made a new constitution in 2011.

THE ECONOMY

A large part of Morocco's **economy** is based on farming. People grow fruits, vegetables, olives, and grains. Morocco's farmers use man-made waterways called canals to bring water to their fields. Farmers also raise sheep and goats. These animals supply meat, wool, and dairy products.

FACT!

Mining is also an important part of Morocco's economy. The country produces minerals such as iron, copper, lead, and zinc.

Moroccan currency, or money, is called dirham.

Fishing is an important job in the country. Morocco sends seafood all over the world.

Morocco's workers make rugs, clothing, and shoes. Factories also make cars, trucks, and other machines people use. Morocco has one of the most successful economies in North Africa.

TOURISM

Morocco's beautiful beaches, mountains, and historic sights make it a popular place for **tourists** to visit. Tourism contributes, or adds, to Morocco's economy and employment. Marrakech, Fès, and Casablanca are just a few of the many places tourists come to see.

Bank Al-Maghrib in Rabat is Morocco's central bank.

THE ENVIRONMENT

Morocco has a Mediterranean **climate**, which is wet in the winter and hot and dry in the summer.

Morocco is home to many animals. Some examples are wild goats, camels, red foxes, desert hares, and the Barbary macaque—a type of monkey. Reptiles and birds live here too.

Olive, eucalyptus, and oak trees dot Morocco's valleys and mountains. Cedar trees grow high in the mountains. Desert plants include cacti, bushes, and herbs. There are 11 national parks in Morocco. Plants and animals within these parks are protected, or kept safe.

NATURAL RESOURCES

Much of Morocco's fuel and electricity comes from oil and gas. However, using different energy sources can save the environment, or the natural world. Morocco is trying to get more of its energy, or power, from sunlight and wind. Waterpower is becoming more common too.

The beautiful waterfall of Akchour is in Talassemtane National Park, Morocco.

FACT!

The Barbary lion is the national animal of Morocco. This animal is native to the Atlas Mountains of North Africa. The last wild Barbary lion was killed in 1922.

Though Barbary lions are extinct (died out) in the wild, some do live in zoos.

THE PEOPLE TODAY

There are around 38 million people living in Morocco today. Moroccans have many different cultural backgrounds. They speak different languages and have different traditions.

FACT!

Many Berbers live in and around the Atlas Mountains.

A Berber man sits outside his house making tea.

Most Moroccans are Arabs or Berbers. These groups have been in Morocco for hundreds of years. Many people also came to Morocco from Spain and Portugal, which are close by.

Long ago, Berbers and Arabs married people from Spain and Portugal. These people became known as Moors. Today, most people don't see Moors as a separate ethnic group.

CASABLANCA

Although Rabat is the capital, Casablanca is the biggest city in Morocco. About 3.9 million people live there. On the shore of the Atlantic Ocean, Casablanca is the main seaport and economic and business center of Morocco.

Casablanca is a man-made port.

LIFESTYLE

Life in Morocco reflects, or shows, a mix of history and modern times. Most Moroccan cities are surrounded by walls. People built these walls hundreds of years ago to keep out enemies. Medinas are old, crowded parts of a city. They're often filled with poor people but also have many people selling items on the street. Souks are market areas. Moroccans shop at souks for fresh foods, spices, and home goods. In cities, people walk or ride motorbikes through the narrow streets.

Many people practice daily prayer **rituals** and wear traditional clothing, such as *kaftans* and *djellabas*.

EDUCATION

Children generally start school when they're 7 years old. They study math, science, history, Islam, and languages. After high school, some students go to college. Others go to schools to learn skills such as carpentry, or woodworking.

Chefchaouen, pictured here, is called the blue city. It's located in the northwest of Morocco.

FACT!

A kaftan is a long garment, or piece of clothing, with long sleeves. A djellaba is a long, loose-fitting robe with a hood.

A man rides his bike through a busy street in Marrakech.

RELIGION

Islam is the main religion, or belief system, in Morocco. Followers of Islam are called Muslims. Islam became Morocco's official religion in the 7th century CE. Muslims follow the teachings of the Prophet Muhammad. They use these teachings in every part of life.

FACT!

Muslims pray five times a day. If they can't make it to the mosque, Muslims can pray anywhere, including at home, school, or work.

Most Moroccans are Sunni Muslims. Sunni Islam is the largest branch of Islam.

Muslims go to a religious building called a mosque. Every city and village in Morocco has one. Mosques have towers called minarets. A man called the muezzin sometimes stands in the minaret to call the faithful to prayer. At a mosque, Muslims pray and listen to teachings from religious leaders called imams.

OTHER RELIGIONS

Ninety-nine percent of people who live in Morocco are Muslim, but there are also small groups of Jewish and Christian people. Most Jewish people live in Rabat and Casablanca.

This is the Muhammad V Mosque in Agadir.

LANGUAGE

Arabic and Berber are the two official languages of Morocco. Arabic is used in school and in business in Morocco. For everyday activities, Moroccans speak a kind of Arabic called Darija.

Berber alphabet letters are pictured here on a blue wall.

FRENCH

Even after Morocco gained independence from France, the French language continued to be widely spoken in Morocco. Although it's not an official language of the country, French can still be heard there today and is often used in business and government. Moroccan children may learn French in school.

There are several Berber languages. The Berber languages have their own alphabet. Sometimes, though, they're written using the Arabic alphabet. Tamazight is the official Berber language spoken in Morocco. Tarifit or Rifian, and Tachelhit are spoken too. The Berber languages are also known as Amazigh languages. Berber people are sometimes called Imazighen.

FACT!

Spanish is also sometimes spoken in Morocco because of the country's closeness to Spain. English is growing in popularity too.

Words of welcome are written in different languages on these blue steps in Chefchaouen.

ARTS AND FESTIVALS

Morocco is home to many different and beautiful forms of art. It's well known for its tilework and **mosaics**. Moroccan fabrics and carpets are also very popular.

Chabbi (or chaabi) is the most popular music in Morocco. It mixes different styles from other countries. Raï, which comes from Algeria, is also popular, and so is hip-hop, which is called hibhub in Morocco.

FACT!
The Marrakech Popular Arts Festival features horsemen riding in traditional clothing.

The Hassan II Mosque in Casablanca has colorful tiles.

Traditional music and dance are a big part of Moroccan festivals. The Fès Festival of World Sacred Music is a nine-day festival that takes place every year, featuring open-air concerts and delicious food.

KALAAT M'GOUNA ROSE FESTIVAL

The Rose Festival is celebrated in Kalaat M'gouna every year in May. This three-day festival is a celebration of the rose **harvest**. It includes traditional music and dances and a rose parade. Thousands of people travel to Morocco to come to the Rose Festival.

These musicians are playing Gnawa music, a mix of African, Arab, and Berber music and dance.

FUN AND PLAY

Horseback riding is both an art and a sport in Morocco. The *tbourida* or *fantasia* festivals feature skillful riders charging, or speeding, on their horses while firing muskets (guns) into the air.

FACT!

Backgammon and chess are popular board games in Morocco. People enjoy playing with friends and family.

This picture shows horsemen charging in the 2019 fantasia event in Casablanca.

Moroccans also play sports on foot. Every year, Morocco hosts the Marathon des Sables, or Sand Marathon. Runners race over 150 miles (240 km) of sand and rocks. It takes seven days to finish the course.

Football, or soccer, is Morocco's most popular sport. Groups of young people play in streets and fields. The Atlas Lions are the national football team of Morocco.

OTHER SPORTS

People who live along the coast of Morocco enjoy different water sports. Swimming, sailing, and surfing are popular. Skiers travel to the Atlas Mountains to enjoy the steep, snowy slopes. People also surf in the desert! They zoom down tall hills of sand on flat boards.

Shown here is a game of soccer on Legzira beach.

FOOD

Moroccan cuisine, or cooking, features many tasty spices, such as cinnamon, cumin, ginger, and saffron. Popular meals include meat and vegetables served with rice or a grain-like food called couscous. Bread is eaten with every meal and is often used to scoop up other food and soak up sauces.

FACT!

Tagine is a special Moroccan stew made of meat and vegetables. It's also the name of the dish in which the meal is served.

People in Morocco love to share food with family and friends.

Moroccans love sweet food. They fill pastries with almonds, dates, and figs and dip them in honey or sugar. Rice pudding with nuts is another popular dessert, and so are different kinds of fruit.

Making and sharing food and drinks is a key part of Moroccan culture and everyday life.

HOSPITALITY

Hospitality is the act of welcoming people and offering them food and drinks. This is an important part of Moroccan culture. The importance of hospitality can be seen clearly in Moroccan tea ceremonies. Serving and sharing tea is a relaxing and enjoyable way to connect with friends old and new.

Mint tea is the most popular drink in Morocco. It's served with every meal.

GLOSSARY

ancient: Very old or belonging to much earlier times.

constitution: The basic laws by which a country, state, or group is governed.

climate: The average weather of a place.

culture: The beliefs and ways of life of a certain group of people.

economy: The way in which goods and services are made, sold, and used in a country or area.

ethnic: Of or relating to large groups of people who have the same cultural background and ways of life.

fertile: Soil or land that's able to produce crops.

harvest: To gather crops after they've grown.

influence: An effect one thing has on another.

mosaic: A picture or pattern produced by arranging together small colored pieces of hard material, such as stone, tile, or glass.

ritual: A religious ceremony, especially one consisting of a series of actions performed in a certain order.

tourist: Someone who travels to visit a place.

tradition: A way of thinking, behaving, or doing something that's been used by people in a particular society for a long time.

FIND OUT MORE

Books

Blech, Rachel. *Fodor's Essential Morocco*. Los Angeles, CA: Fodor's Travel Publications, 2022.

Ranger, Helen, Sarah Gilbert, Sally Kirby, Mandy Sinclair, Tara Stevens. *Lonely Planet Morocco*. Oakland, CA: Lonely Planet Publishing, 2023.

York, Jillian C. *Morocco: The Essential Guide to Customs and Culture*. London, UK: Kuperard Publishers 2023.

Websites

Britannica: Morocco
www.britannica.com/place/Morocco
Learn more about Morocco's history.

Lonely Planet: Morocco
www.lonelyplanet.com/morocco
Learn more about all there is to see and do in Morocco.

Video

Region of Craftwork - Artisanat Marrakech
www.youtube.com/watch?v=U8Iaz17HT9I
Watch artisans at work in Marrakech.

Publisher's note to educators and parents: Our editors have carefully reviewed these websites to ensure that they are suitable for students. Many websites change frequently, however, and we cannot guarantee that a site's future contents will continue to meet our high standards of quality and educational value. Be advised that students should be closely supervised whenever they access the internet.

INDEX

A
agriculture, 12, 25
Arab people, 5, 8, 17, 25
arts, 5, 24, 25
Atlantic Ocean, 4, 17
Atlas Mountains, 7, 15, 27

B
Berber people, 5, 8, 16, 17, 22, 23, 25

C
climate/weather, 14
clothing, 18, 19
cuisine, 4, 5, 25, 28, 29

E
economy, 12, 13, 17
education, 10, 18, 22

G
government, 10, 11, 22

H
Hafid, Abd al- (sultan), 9
Hassan II (king), 8, 9

L
language, 5, 16, 18, 22, 23

M
Mediterranean Sea, 4, 7
Moulouya River, 7
Muhammad (prophet), 20
Muḥammad V (sultan), 9
Muḥammad VI (king), 8

P
plants, 14

R
religion, 5, 18, 20, 21
Rif mountains, 7

S
Sahara desert, 6
Sahrawi people, 7
sports, 5, 27
Strait of Gibraltar, 6

T
tourism, 13

W
Western Sahara, 6, 7
wildlife, 14, 15